Girls
IN THE LEAD

By Alissa Norby

youth light inc.

© 2008 by YouthLight, Inc.
Chapin, SC 29036

Cover Design and Layout by Diane Florence
Project Editing by Susan Bowman

ISBN: 978-1-59850-050-9

Library of Congress Number
2007943873

10 9 8 7 6 5 4 3 2 1
Printed in the United States

Acknowledgements

I would like to first and foremost thank my parents for their unconditional support during this process. From listening to my seemingly never-ending rants on relational aggression to bringing me tea when I am stressed, you have been there for me 100%. Special thanks to Sally Wendt for encouraging my exploration, Joyce Devlin for showing me that I have insight to bring to the theatre world, Bonnie Wade for the constant inspiration, Nikki Patin for challenging me to look deeper into these issues, and Toylee Green-Harris for giving me so many opportunities. Thanks to all of the schools and organizations I have worked with in the past few years- I have learned so much! I feel truly blessed to have been able to work with such amazing counselors, social workers, faculty, and staff. Thanks to Cheryl and Gretchen for our discussions; I am constantly in awe of you two. Thanks to all of my incredible friends for your love and support. You are simply irreplaceable. Thanks to Lisa for keeping me sane (well, as sane as possible) and for believing that I can create change. Thanks to the Bowmans for your invaluable support and belief in this project. And finally, many thanks to all of the girls I have worked with—you continue to inspire me everyday.

Dedication

This is for all girls who have ever struggled with this issue. To the mothers, sisters, grandmothers, aunts, teachers, counselors, and friends who have been there. To those of you whom I have worked with and those of you I have yet to meet: I believe that we have the power to change this. Your courage, strength, and resiliency will forever be a source of inspiration.

Table of Contents

Introduction 6

The Need for this Book 6

Why Theatre? 6

How to Use This Book 7

Girls in the Lead Permission Slip 10

Session 1:

GETTING TO KNOW YOU: *Group Introduction* **11**

    Pre-Program Surveys 11

    Activity 1: Tossin' It Up 12

    Activity 2: Jingo Bingo 13

    Activity 3: The Real Deal 14

Session 2:

START OF SOMETHING NEW: *Building Group Trust* **15**

    Free-Write 15

    Activity 4: Creating the Rules 16

    Activity 5: Blindfolded Landmine 17

Session 3:

GET'CHA HEAD IN THE GAME: *Introduction to Relational Aggression* **18**

    Free-Write 18

    Activity 6: Freeze! 19

    Activity 7: Storytellers 20

Session 4:

WELCOME TO THE JUNGLE: *What's Going on at School* **21**

    Free-Write 21

    Activity 8: Time Dash! 22

Session 5:

YOU ARE THE WIND BENEATH MY WINGS…SORT OF: *Friends and Cliques* **23**

    Free-Write 23

    Group Discussion 24

    Activity 10: Party Animals 25

    Activity 11: The Best Girl for the Job 26

Session 6:

THE BIRDS AND THE BEES THEY DIDN'T TELL YOU: *Exploring Gender Dynamics* **27**

    Free-Write 27

    Activity 12: What's in a Name? 28

    Activity 13: Flip-Flop! 29

Table of Contents

Session 7:
TAKING CARE OF BUSINESS PT. 1: *Learning Empathy, Understanding, and Context*...................**30**
Free-Write 30
Activity 14: Makin' Faces 1 31
Activity 15: The Voice Inside My Head 32

Session 8:
TAKING CARE OF BUSINESS PT. 2: *Learning Empathy, Understanding, and Context*...................**33**
Group Discussion 33
Activity 16: Objection!...36

Session 9:
SEE WHAT I WANNA SEE: *Media Literacy* **37**
Free-Write 37
Group Discussion 37
Activity 17: And Now a Word From Our Sponsors! 39
Activity 18: Theatrical Trailer 40

Session 10:
HOW TO DEAL PT. 1: *Healing and Dealing*..**41**
Free-Write 41
Activity 19: Pick Up Lines!...42
Activity 20: The Tough Stuff 43
Activity 21: Every Other Line 44
At Home Activity 44

Session 11:
HOW TO DEAL PT. 2: *Healing and Dealing*..**45**
Free-Write 45
Group Discussion 45
Activity 22: Stay or Go?...47
Final Project 47

Session 12:
WE'RE ALL IN THIS TOGETHER: *Saying Goodbye* **48**
Final Project 48
Post-Program Surveys..49
Celebration/Goodbye 49

Optional Session 1:
TAKING CARE OF BUSINESS PT. 3: *An Exercise in Empathy*...**51**
Activity 23: Power Hop 52
Activity 24: What's in a Name? 53
Activity 25: Star Power 54

Optional Session 2:

TTYL: *Saying 'Talk to you Later' to Cyberbullying* **56**
    Activity 26: Freeze Frame 57
    Activity 27: Splat! 58
    Activity 28: Mano-a-Mano 59

Optional Session 3:

BEST OF BOTH WORLDS?: *Exploring Sexual Violence, Sexuality, and Stigma* **60**
    Activity 29: Reputation Heads Up 7 Up 61
    Activity 30: Makin Faces 2 62
    Activity 31: Dating Bill of Rights 63

    Pre- and Post- Program Survey Sheets 64
    Jingo Bingo Activity Sheet..66
    The Best Girl for the Job Questionnaire 67
    Makin' Faces 1 Activity: Scenarios 68
    Stay or Go? Scenarios..69
    Power Hop Statements...70
    Star Power Activity Cut-Out 71
    Makin' Faces 2 Activity: Scenarios 72
    Dating Bill of Rights Activity Sheet 73
    Clique Break-Down 74

Alternate Activities...**75**

Girls in the Lead Certificate of Completion...**79**

Girls in the Lead Thank-You Card..**81**

Bibliography and Recommended Reading...**82**

About the Author **83**

Introduction

The Need for this Book

Relational Aggression, or covert and indirect bullying has become one of the biggest problems facing schools and communities today. I have been able to witness this firsthand through my work as a school consultant, program director, and as a woman myself. From the earliest devastation of losing that first friend to the more intense struggle for self, she will experience in her later years, relational aggression and peer conflict play an important and often damaging role in a girl's life. This issue affects us all; whether we are a parent, teacher, administrator, friend, family, or clergy member. The number one question I hear from each of you is what we can practically do to start eradicating this problem; and I have spent the last several years trying to find an answer. You are now holding it in your hands. *Girls in the Lead* is an easy-to-follow, hands-on curriculum filled with the most effective activities and exercises I have found that help girls learn to deal with conflict in a healthy and productive way. The intent of *Girls in the Lead* is to aid girls in understanding and exploring the dynamics of friends, relationships, and conflict. The program challenges girls to figure out how to resolve issues in a positive and constructive manner.

Why Theatre?

I have been working with girls in various capacities for a number of years now and I constantly find that girls respond very well to improvisational games and other theatre activities. The theatre games I have used in my work with girls always proved to be the most effective and influential of all my exercises. Anyone who has worked with girls knows how much they love to go up onstage and create skits, but I believe there is more to it than that. Theatre allows us to observe ourselves and others in action. This program helps girls reflect on themselves, their behavior and their thoughts. Girls will see themselves today and imagine themselves tomorrow. Everything that actors do, they do throughout their own lives; therefore, when I ask a group of girls to come up with a skit that involves relational aggression, they are not just playing "characters"— they are playing themselves. Girls put into a character what they may feel too defensive and vulnerable to admit to or talk about themselves. This not only helps the group leader gain knowledge of what is taking place at school, but it allows the girls to reflect on their own behavior- to see what is reality, but also to explore what is possibility. Therefore, the activities are not designed to be dogmatic; they are not intended to preach to the girls about what they should be doing, but rather allow them to come up with their own solutions. The program is named *Girls in the Lead* because of this. Through this curriculum, girls will figure out and discover their own ways to deal with conflict in a healthy manner, as opposed to the adult facilitator telling the group what the answers should be. It has been my experience that, if you allow girls this freedom, they will eventually discover the same answers and lessons that we wish to teach them. Many of the activities specifically enable girls to explore their world as it is, why it is thus, and how it can be changed. *Girls in the Lead* will help girls build this future, rather than just waiting for it.

How to Use this Book

An Introduction

Girls in the Lead is intended first and foremost to help girls understand the dynamics of relational aggression, or covert and indirect social bullying. The curriculum will allow you as the group facilitator to help the girls find ways to prevent and intervene in cases of female bullying and victimization. *Girls in the Lead* is specifically designed to help girls develop an understanding of how to resolve conflict in healthy, positive, and pro-active ways.

Girls in the Lead can be used by professional school counselors, teachers, social workers, psychologists, administrators, and/or any others who work with groups of adolescent girls and who wish to bring about change in the way young women relate to one another.

This book consists of eleven 60-minute sessions that will help you and your school or organization accomplish these goals. *Girls in the Lead* also comes with optional sessions and activities, most intended for older-aged girls, which you may use at your discretion. You will also find pre/post surveys, a group evaluation form to measure success, additional activities and handouts, journal topics, and insightful instruction in this book. Each session focuses on a set of specific issues that builds on the previous day's topics.

The *Girls in the Lead* curriculum is meant to be used with a small group of girls, consisting of anywhere from 10-15 participants. However, it is easily adaptable to both smaller and larger groups.

What You Will Need

- Writing journal for each girl
- Scrap paper
- Pens and pencils
- Poster board
- Three balls of any shape or size
- Scissors
- Tissue Box
- Hat or bowl

Pre- and Post- Program Surveys

The pre- and post- program surveys (see back of book) should be distributed and completed during the first and final group session, respectively. Once turned in, these surveys will help you, your school, and/or organization measure the effectiveness of the *Girls in the Lead* program.

How to Use this Book

Group Evaluation Form

The group evaluation form (see back of book) should be distributed to each member of the group roughly two to four weeks following the end of the program. This evaluation form is intended for you, your school, and/or organization to measure the success of the *Girls in the Lead* program. The evaluation also serves to review the progress the girls have made as a result of participating in group. If possible, invite the group back to discuss and evaluate the program and to check-in on the girls' individual progress.

Thank-You Cards

I recommend making personalized thank-you cards for each girl in your group upon her completion of the program. This is a terrific way to end the program, as it will give each girl a sense of personal accomplishment and pride. A reproducible *Girls in the Lead* Thank-You Card can be found in the back of this book.

Drop-Box

The Drop-Box is a small box in which group participants can place confidential questions or concerns. I recommend decorating a small tissue box, but any sized or shaped box should suffice. Explain to the girls that if there is something they wish to speak to you about in private, they should write it down on a piece of paper and put it in the Drop-Box. Make sure to go through and empty the Drop-Box after each session and address any issues privately and as you see fit.

Group Discussions

The group discussions are designed to help your group target specific issues in a more in-depth manner. These discussions also help to build group trust and cohesiveness. In addition, each individual group topic comes with its own specific set of instructions to make the group discussion as effective as possible. While conducting a group discussion, remember to encourage participation from all girls; this will help in establishing trust and comfort in the program.

Free-Writes

Each girl should have her own journal in which to complete all of the "Free-Writes." "Free-Writes" are journal topics that the girls should finish at the beginning of each session. Journaling will establish a calm and reflective environment each time your group meets, and will also help to facilitate the girls' understanding and exploration of the various topics addressed in the sessions.

How to Use this Book

Shout Outs!

"Shout Outs!" is the time at the end of the group when the girls should compliment each other for the work they have done that day. Each girl should give every other girl a "Shout Out!" for each session. For example, if a girl noticed that another group member took a leadership role in one of the activities, the girl would give her a "Shout Out!" for that. This helps the group wind down and leave with an overall feeling of accomplishment.

The 411

"The 411" boxes are meant to provide you with additional understanding of each activity and its objective.

Step Up!

The "Step Up!" boxes are meant to provide you with additional instruction and tips for the activities. These tips come from my own personal experience working with girls and are meant to help you facilitate and direct activities more effectively.

Cool Q's

The "Cool Q's" boxes provide you with discussion questions to ask the group after the activity. Holding these discussions will make sure that the girls have gained as much understanding and growth from the activity as possible.

Permission Slip

I give my daughter, _____ permission to attend and participate in the Girls in the Lead program. I understand that the mission of this program is to help my daughter and other girls develop empathy, prevent gossip and bullying, and learn healthy conflict resolution skills. I also understand that my daughter may miss a small portion of class time in order to attend the Girls in the Lead sessions.

_____
Parent/Guardian Signature

_____
Date

Session 1

GETTING TO KNOW YOU:
Group Introduction

The first day should always be about getting to know the girls, and more importantly, helping the girls to get to know each other. After introducing and explaining what the *Girls in the Lead* program is and what the girls can expect from it, encourage the girls to start building relationships with each other. This session will help set the tone for the rest of the program.

Group Check-In

Gather the girls together, sit in a circle. Introduce yourself, tell them why you are here, what the *Girls in the Lead* program is, and what they can expect from the coming weeks:
- Explain that this is a safe space, and what that means. For instance, what is said in the group, stays in the group.
- Explain how each session will begin with a journal entry, or "free write," to help the girls start brainstorming and reflecting on various issues that affect them.
- Explain "Shout Outs!", the time at the end of the day when we give each other compliments or encouragement based on what happened at the session (e.g. if Amanda, a shy girl, finally speaks up about something that is really important to her, someone would give her a "Shout Out" for that).
- Explain the Drop-Box and encourage the girls to use it.

Pre-Program Surveys

- *The 411*
  This survey will help you understand some of the basic issues and conflicts that the girls deal with, and more importantly, how they deal with them.
- *Materials*
  Pre-Program Survey on page 64
  Pencils/pens
- *Instructions*
  Distribute a pre-program survey to each girl along with a pen or other writing utensil. Collect these from the girls when they are finished.
- *Step Up!*
  Be sure to remind the girls that you, the instructor, will be the only one to see these surveys. Therefore, they should be as honest as possible when answering the questions.

Activity 1: Tossin' It Up

The 411

This game is intended for the girls to learn to connect with one and listen to one another.

Materials

Three balls of any shape or size.

Instructions

First, ask the girls to each share their names, ages, a "fun fact" about themselves, and why they are here. Then ask the girls to form a circle and choose one girl who will start with the ball. She then says another participant's name, looks at her, and throws the ball to this participant. Now the girl who just received the ball should throw it, in the same manner, to another group member. This continues until the ball has reached everyone in the room (always with the name said first, then the ball thrown). Ask the girls to memorize this order of names. Now, set the first ball aside, and add the second. Follow the same steps with the second ball, except the order in which the ball is thrown should change. Once the girls have this one down, ask them to do the first pattern again with the first ball. In the middle of this pattern, start the second pattern with the second ball. Therefore, the girls will be throwing two different balls, with two different name patterns, at the same time. Finally, if you are daring enough, throw in that third ball!

Step Up!

The game will inevitably make the girls feel frustrated (balls will drop, people will forget where to throw the ball), so make sure you help the girls realize that they need to go slowly, patiently, and with attention. By encouraging this, you are setting up a great group dynamic for the rest of the program.

Cool Q's

- What made this game challenging?
- What could help you complete this game more quickly and efficiently?

Activity 2: Jingo-Bingo

The 411

This activity helps the girls to get to know one another and establish connections with each other.

Materials

- Jingo-Bingo sheets on page 66
- Pens or pencils

Instructions

Distribute a Jingo Bingo sheet to each girl along with a pen or pencil. Tell the girls that they must find members of the group who match with each Jingo Bingo square's instructions. When you give the sign to start, the girls will be able to move around the room and attempt to fill out their grids, finding a different girl's name to fill each square. The first girl to fill her entire grid wins.

Step Up!

Make sure to discourage fierce competition during this activity. Remember: This exercise is about the girls getting to know one another, not competing against one another.

Cool Q's

- Did you learn anything interesting about someone else in group?
- Did you find you shared anything in common with another girl?
- Did you find anything surprising?

Activity 3: The Real Deal

The 411

This is a fun activity designed to help girls get to know one another and discover new facts about each other.

Instructions

Ask the girls to form a circle. Each girl gives three statements about herself; two must be true and one must be a lie. Then, ask the rest of the group to vote on which is the false statement. The girl then reveals the answer.

Shout Outs!

End the day by circling the girls up, and having the girls give "Shout Outs" to one another. Each girl should give at least one compliment or kudos for the day to every other girl. Thank the girls for coming.

Session 2

START OF SOMETHING NEW:
Building Group Trust

The primary purpose of the second day is much like the first: encourage the girls to get to know one another and to be comfortable around each other. This session is about teamwork and building trust- not igniting competition. This session will also help to create a safe space environment.

Group Check-In

Gather the girls into a comfortable circle or grouping and ask them about their week, how things are going at school; if there have been any issues lately, etc.

Free-Write

Distribute journals. Allow girls to write about a topic of their choice.

Activity 4: Creating the Rules

The 411

Allowing the girls to create their own rules shows them not only that you trust them, but that you view them as competent young women. Therefore, the girls will be more inclined to follow the rules that they, themselves, have created.

Materials

- Dry erase board or poster board
- Markers

Instructions

Ask the girls to create a list of rules that they will have to abide by for the remaining weeks. Record these rules on a board for the entire group to see. At the end, have each girl come to the board and sign her name at the bottom.

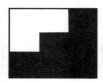

Step Up!

In case the girls do not suggest it, make sure to add rules such as confidentiality, respect, honesty, and the "right to pass."

Cool Q's

- Are these rules realistic? Do you think you could follow them?
- What will be hard about following these rules?
- What can we do to help each other follow these rules?

Activity 5: Blindfolded Landmine

The 411

This activity is designed to build group trust and cohesiveness while helping the girls to become comfortable with one another.

Materials

- Several pieces of paper or other objects

Instructions

Scatter the paper and/or objects around the room. Ask the girls to group themselves into pairs and select one to be the "driver" and the other the "passenger." The "passenger" will close her eyes and start walking around the room. The "driver" will help steer her, or move her around, to avoid hitting the objects (as if in an obstacle course). After a while, have the girls switch roles.

Step Up!

This activity is about both physical and mental trust. Encourage the girls to be as trusting and daring in their movements as possible. If time permits, ask the girls to repeat the exercise with different partners.

Cool Q's

- What did you like about this activity? What was fun?
- What challenged you in this activity?

Shout Outs!

End the day by circling the girls up, and having the girls give "Shout Outs" to one another. Each girl should give at least one compliment or kudos for the day to every other girl. Thank the girls for coming.

Session 3

GET'CHA HEAD IN THE GAME: Introduction to Relational Aggression

This is the "dive-in" day. The girls will start discussing relational aggression, female bullying, and day-to-day conflicts and issues that they encounter. All of the activities are designed to help the girls begin to open up about their experiences.

Group Check-In

Gather the girls into a comfortable circle or grouping and ask them about their week, how things are going at school; if there have been any issues lately, etc.

Free-Write

"What is the most hurtful fight you have ever been in with a friend? What was the situation? What led to it? What was the outcome?"

Whoosh!

Gather the girls in a circle. Select someone to begin and instruct her to either make a noise, a gesture, a movement or all three at the same time. As quickly as possible, each girl, starting to the right, will imitate her action(s) until her "Whoosh" goes all the way around the circle once. The next girl to the right will then create her own "Whoosh" and send it around the circle. This continues until everyone has the opportunity to create their own individual "Whoosh."

Step Up!

This is the standard warm-up that the girls will be doing at the beginning of most sessions. It helps to energize the group, especially if you are meeting after school. With this in mind, always make sure to encourage enthusiasm, creativity, and participation.

Activity 6: Freeze!

The 411

This activity will not just help the girls explore relational aggression, it will help you to gain an initial understanding of the types of bullying commonly seen in your school.

Instructions

Two girls take the stage, and start to improvise a scene about bullying (e.g. two girls in a fight, a rumor being spread around school, etc.). When the scene reaches a climax, or end, another girl from the audience should call out "Freeze!," and the two players onstage must freeze in place and pause the scene. The girl from the audience then goes up onstage and 'tags' one of these players out of the scene (usually by tapping her). The tagged player should then have a seat, and the girl who shouted "Freeze!" should assume this player's exact physical ending position (or how she looked frozen). Then, the new girl onstage starts a new scene about bullying with the remaining player.

Step Up!

If you start to see the same scenes over and over, encourage the girls to vary them.

Cool Q's

- What were these scenes about? What did you see?
- Were there any common storylines throughout?

Activity 7: Storytellers

The 411

This exercise is designed to help the girls reflect on their experiences with bullying at school while also helping you, as the group leader, understand what some of these instances look like.

Instructions

Gather the girls into a circle. Ask them to tell a story about a typical fight, or conflict, between two good friends. One girl should start by telling the first sentence of the story. Then, the girl sitting to her right will tell the next sentence of the story, and so forth. This way, the group, as a whole, develops the story sentence by sentence and person by person.

Cool Q's

- How realistic was this story? How realistic was the outcome of the story?
- Was there resolution between/among friends? Why or why not?
- Did everyone agree on where the story should go? Why or why not?
- Has anything like the story ever happened to you, or a friend of yours?

Shout Outs!

End the day by circling the girls up, and having the girls give "Shout Outs" to one another. Each girl should give at least one compliment or kudos for the day to every other girl. Thank the girls for coming.

Session 4

WELCOME TO THE JUNGLE:
What's Going on at School

This day is meant to build on the last session; that is, the activities dig deeper into the friendship issues and conflicts that the girls face at school. The activities are designed to help the girls begin to explore and understand why they behave the way they do, and to help you understand this as well.

Group Check-In

Gather the girls into a comfortable circle or grouping and ask them about their week, how things are going at school; if there have been any issues lately, etc.

Free-Write

"What is the most common reason two friends get into a fight, or have a falling-out?"

Whoosh!

Gather the girls in a circle. Select someone to begin and instruct her to either make a noise, a gesture, a movement or all three at the same time. As quickly as possible, each girl, starting to the right, will imitate her action(s) until her "Whoosh" goes all the way around the circle once. The next girl to the right will then create her own "Whoosh" and send it around the circle. This continues until everyone has the opportunity to create their own individual "Whoosh."

Activity 8: Time Dash!

The 411

This activity is specifically designed to help the girls understand how small disagreements and misunderstandings can be blown out of proportion, thus causing bigger fights and problems between friends.

Instructions

Encourage the girls to think about a situation with a friend, or friends, which would inspire a strong emotion in them. Then ask each girl to walk around the room and express this emotion through her face and body. For instance, maybe a girl looks sad because her friends are excluding her; maybe a girl is happy because she and her best friend just made up after a fight. Then, after about one minute, ask the girls to freeze in place. Go around to each girl and ask her why she is exhibiting that specific expression, i.e. what happened to make her feel that way.

Step Up!

Make sure to encourage honesty and creativity during this exercise. If the girls feel uncomfortable performing alone, have them do this activity in pairs.

Shout Outs!

End the day by circling the girls up, and having the girls give "Shout Outs" to one another. Each girl should give at least one compliment or kudos for the day to every other girl. Thank the girls for coming.

Session 5

YOU ARE THE WIND BENEATH MY WINGS ... SORT OF:
Friends and Cliques

This session encourages the girls to explore and understand the dynamics in different cliques and relationships. It will also help you understand what types of cliques are ruling your school. Most importantly, the activities are designed to challenge the girls to really think about what types of relationships they would ideally like to have versus what types of relationships they actually have.

Group Check-In

Gather the girls into a comfortable circle or grouping and ask them about their week, how things are going at school; if there have been any issues lately, etc.

Free-Write

"What do you think a clique is? What have you heard about them? What kind of people make up a clique?"

Step Up!

If girls are uncomfortable writing about their own clique, ask them to write about what they see at school. If they are uncomfortable with this, ask the girls to write about what they see in movies, television, etc.

Whoosh!

Gather the girls in a circle. Select someone to begin and instruct her to either make a noise, a gesture, a movement or all three at the same time. As quickly as possible, each girl, starting to the right, will imitate her action(s) until her "Whoosh" goes all the way around the circle once. The next girl to the right will then create her own "Whoosh" and send it around the circle. This continues until everyone has the opportunity to create their own individual "Whoosh."

...(continued)

YOU ARE THE WIND BENEATH MY WINGS ... SORT OF:
Friends and Cliques

Group Discussion

- *The 411*
  This group discussion topic is designed to help girls understand the social roles and social hierarchies that they create or observe at school. The girls will also learn about the behavior expectations that come with feeling trapped in a certain role.

- *Materials*
  Poster board
  Markers or pens

- *Instructions*
  Ask girls the question and allow them to freely provide their own answers and feelings on the topic. Record their answers on poster board. Use "Cool Qs" for further discussion.

- *Step Up!*
  The main roles in a clique that you want the group to understand are: Queen Bee (leader, main aggressor), Wannabe (second-in-command to Queen Bee), Bystanders (those who stand by and watch the agression), and Targets (victims of the aggression). See Clique Break-Down on page 74 for more assistance.

- *Cool Q's*
  What kinds of cliques or groups do you typically see at school?
  Are the roles clear-cut?
  Do girls ever change roles?
  What is good about a clique? What is bad?

Activity 10: Party Animals

The 411

This activity teaches the girls about the different roles people play in cliques and other social hierarchies. It will help them recognize the signs and behaviors of each of these roles.

Instructions

Separate the girls into groups of four. Each group should then choose one person to play the role of party host. Have the party host leave the group while the other three girls each choose to play the role of either queen bee, wannabe, bystander or target. The Party Host should not know which of the three players is playing each role. The group will then improvise a scene that takes place at a party. The three players attend the party, and through dialogue with these players, the Party Host must determine who is playing which one. At the end of the scene, the Party Host must give her guess, and the players should reveal the correct answers.

Step Up!

This exercise can be a great deal of fun, but it can quickly turn chaotic and silly. Make sure to encourage the girls to take it seriously, and to play their roles as sincerely as possible. Also, be sure to instruct the girl playing Party Host to ask the players questions about how each would act in a friendship or relationship; this will help her determine the roles more quickly.

Cool Q's

- How can you tell if someone is a Queen Bee, Wannabe, Bystander, or Target?
- What separates them?
- How does a girl know who is who in her own group?
- Is it possible to change roles?

Activity 11: The Best Girl for the Job

The 411

This activity helps the girls see that their ideal friend does not always match up with the friends that they actually have. The girls will realize that sometimes they may compromise their values and expectations in order to feel included or popular.

Materials

The Best Girl for the Job Questionnaire on page 67

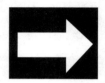

Instructions

This activity is exactly like the reality show dating games seen on television. However, instead of picking a significant other, the girls will be picking a best friend. Ask girls to get into groups of five. One girl in each group will be playing the role of the "Bachelorette" (or the one looking for a friend), while the others will play the Queen Bee, the Wannabe, the Bystander, and the Good Friend. Once the Bachelorette is chosen, instruct the four remaining girls to pick the role they wish to play, but have them do this away from the Bachelorette. The girl playing the Bachelorette should not be aware of who is playing which role; the girls should introduce themselves as Contestant #1, #2, #3, and #4. Provide each Bachelorette with the Best Girl for the Job Questionnaire on page 67. She will then ask each question from the list and each of the contestants will have to answer honestly, as the character would in real life, but with their backs turned to the Bachelorette. The Bachelorette will then reveal which contestant (either #1, #2, #3, or #4) she would like as a friend. Finally, whichever contestant was chosen should reveal what role she was playing.

Cool Q's

- Why did you pick who you did?
- What qualities did each character have?
- What qualities do you value in a friend?
- Do you ever feel like your friends don't have these values?

Shout Outs!

End the day by circling the girls up, and having the girls give "Shout Outs" to one another. Each girl should give at least one compliment or kudos for the day to every other girl. Thank the girls for coming.

THE BIRDS AND THE BEES THEY DIDN'T TELL YOU: *Exploring Gender Dynamics*

This session will help the girls understand the difference in the ways males and females build relationships and deal with conflict.

Group Check-In

Gather the girls into a comfortable circle or grouping and ask them about their week, how things are going at school; if there have been any issues lately, etc.

Free-Write

"How do boys fight with one another? How do they interact, versus how we interact? What privileges do boys have that we don't?"

Whoosh!

Gather the girls in a circle. Select someone to begin and instruct her to either make a noise, a gesture, a movement or all three at the same time. As quickly as possible, each girl, starting to the right, will imitate her action(s) until her "Whoosh" goes all the way around the circle once. The next girl to the right will then create her own "Whoosh" and send it around the circle. This continues until everyone has the opportunity to create their own individual "Whoosh."

Activity 12: What's in a Name?

The 411

This activity will help the girls begin to understand the different expectations for both men and women in our culture and how these affect the way we all interact and deal with conflict.

Materials

Poster board
Pens or markers

Instructions

On the first poster board, write "Girls"; on the second, write "Boys." Hand out a marker or pen to each girl, and ask them to think of names that they typically associate with boys versus names that they associate with girls. Then, ask the group to write these names on the appropriate posters. Once this is done, ask the girls to go back up and write the different privileges that they feel each gender is entitled to. Finally, ask the girls to go up a third time and write a "+" next to the positive names and privileges, and a "—" next to the negative ones.

Step Up!

The "names" should not be birth-names such as John or Sarah, but rather descriptive names for boys and girls (e.g. brat, or thug). Allow the girls to write whatever names they feel are appropriate.

Cool Q's

- Which names were negative? Which were positive? Why?
- What privileges do boys have that you wish you had?
- Why is it that we mainly have negative names to refer to women? Why do boys have mainly positive names?
- How do you think all of this affects our relationships or the way we handle fights?

Activity 13: Flip-Flop!

The 411

This exercise helps the girls explore how boys and girls deal with conflict differently. Most likely you will find that the girls feel that boys are able to work things out faster and are less likely to hold grudges.

Instructions

Separate the girls into pairs. Each pair will act out a scene where one girl is either bullying the other or is fighting with her. Have the girls act out the beginning, middle, and end/outcome of the conflict. Then, the girls will change "masks"—they will act out the exact same scene (same plot) but as boys experiencing this conflict instead of girls.

Step Up!

This activity can become silly and crazy very quickly, so remember to encourage the girls to really think about their choices and to take these scenes as seriously as possible.

Cool Q's

- What were some of the differences when the scene flip-flopped?
- Do boys hold onto grudges?
- Are girls immediately friends after a fight?
- What do girls normally fight about? What about boys?

Shout Outs!

End the day by circling the girls up, and having the girls give "Shout Outs" to one another. Each girl should give at least one compliment or kudos for the day to every other girl. Thank the girls for coming.

Session 7

TAKING CARE OF BUSINESS PT.1: *Learning Empathy, Understanding, and Context*

The "Taking Care of Business" sessions are meant to help girls explore why they fight the way that they do and how these behaviors can be changed. This is the key time for you, as the group leader, to help them understand that there are reasons for what we do, but there is also room to better ourselves.

Group Check-In

Gather the girls into a comfortable circle or grouping and ask them about their week, how things are going at school; if there have been any issues lately, etc.

Free-Write

"Has a friend ever thought you were mad at her, when in reality you were cool with her? Or vice versa? What wound up happening in the end?"

Whoosh!

Gather the girls in a circle. Select someone to begin and instruct her to either make a noise, a gesture, a movement or all three at the same time. As quickly as possible, each girl, starting to the right, will imitate her action(s) until her "Whoosh" goes all the way around the circle once. The next girl to the right will then create her own "Whoosh" and send it around the circle. This continues until everyone has the opportunity to create their own individual "Whoosh."

Activity 14: Makin' Faces 1

The 411

This activity is designed to help girls understand that, just because someone might have an unhappy look on her face, it does not necessarily mean that she is angry with you. Girls frequently misinterpret their friends' behaviors and expressions, which in turn causes fights to erupt. This activity will combat these instances.

Materials

Makin' Faces 1: Scenarios sheet on page 68
Hat or bowl
Scissors

Instructions

Cut-out and place Makin' Faces 1 scenarios into the hat or bowl. Separate the girls into pairs and have each pair come up to the performance area one at a time. One girl in the pair will pick out a slip of paper, or scenario, from "the hat" and read it to herself. The girls will then act out a simple and silent scene in which two girls walk past each other in the hallway. The girl who picked up the piece of paper will express the evoked emotion from the scenario on her face without saying anything while she walks past the other. Observe the reaction of the second girl and ask her; is she angry? Upset? Does she think the other girl is mad at her? Jealous, maybe? What will she do about it? Next, ask the first girl to read her scenario out loud to the group. This way, the girl learns that the expression that might have seemed sour had absolutely nothing to do with her, despite what she may have assumed.

Step Up!

Encourage the girls to take their time with this exercise, and to really think about the expression they're creating or viewing, and how it makes them feel.

Cool Q's

- What was it like to be in that scene? How was everyone feeling?
- Were you surprised to hear the "real" story? Had you already jumped to conclusions?
- Have you ever had an experience where you have misread someone, or vice-versa?

Activity 15: The Voice Inside My Head

The 411
This activity is meant to encourage girls to examine what they think and feel, versus what they say while in a conflict. It will help the group explore why we, as women, lie instead of being honest in a confrontation with a friend.

Instructions
Separate the girls into groups of four. Two will act out a scene, while the other two will play "their inner voices." Have group members decide who will be playing which roles. Then ask each group to develop a scene that centers around one friend confronting another about a problem, or two girls who are having a fight. The two girls will act out the scene, while "their inner voices" will say what each character is really thinking (or what she really wants to say).

> Example:
> Character1: "Why didn't you invite me to your birthday party?"
> Voice1: "Yeah…why didn't she? Does she not like me anymore?"
> Character2: "Oh, my mom wouldn't let me."
> Voice2: "Actually…my friends just think she's a loser."

Step Up!
Encourage the girls to be patient and to go through their lines slowly, especially the girls who are playing "the voices." These girls should really take the time to think about what they would be feeling or thinking after each line of dialogue. This way, the lines that represent the girls' thoughts will be as honest and realistic as possible.

Cool Q's
- Has a situation like this ever happened to you?
- When, and why, do you not say what you mean?
- What happens when you don't say what you really feel?
- Do girls typically confront each other? How?

Shout Outs!

End the day by circling the girls up, and having the girls give "Shout Outs" to one another. Each girl should give at least one compliment or kudos for the day to every other girl. Thank the girls for coming.

Session 8

TAKING CARE OF BUSINESS PT.2: *Learning Empathy, Understanding, and Context*

Group Check-In

Gather the girls into a comfortable circle or grouping and ask them about their week, how things are going at school; if there have been any issues lately, etc.

Whoosh!

Gather the girls in a circle. A person starts by doing a noise, a gesture, movement, or all three at the same time. Once she does this, it is passed along the circle as fast as possible (each subsequent participant imitates it), until it reaches its creator. Then the next person, to the right, creates her own "Whoosh." This continues until everyone in the circle has had the opportunity to create their own individual "Whoosh."

Group Discussion

"What is the difference between joking and taunting?"

- *The 411*
  This group discussion topic will help girls examine the difference between playful joking and verbal harassment. A better understanding of these two behaviors will help girls understand when and how to report different situations depending on their severity.

- *Materials*
  Poster board
  Markers or pens

- *Instructions*
  Ask girls the question and allow them to freely provide their own answers and feelings on the topic. Record their answers on poster board. Use "Cool Qs" for further discussion.

| 33

Session 8

TAKING CARE OF BUSINESS PT.2: *Learning Empathy, Understanding, and Context*

- *Step Up!*
  Explain that it is normal, and not at all shameful, to be hurt or confused by comments that are ambiguous in nature and/or tone. Although friends joke and poke fun at each other, it is only okay when both girls understand that it is just joking, and not a wolf in sheep's clothing.

- *Cool Q's*
  How do you know when someone is joking?
  Do girls ever mix these two up?
  What should you do if someone is taunting you?

Group Discussion

"What is the difference between sharing and gossiping?"

- *The 411*
  This group discussion topic will help girls understand the very crucial difference between sharing information for safety reasons versus gossiping out of spite or interest in personal gain.

- *Materials*
  Poster board
  Markers or pens

- *Instructions*
  Ask girls the question and allow them to freely provide their own answers and feelings on the topic. Record their answers on poster board. Use "Cool Qs" for further discussion.

- *Step Up!*
  Help the girls understand that sometimes, if the situation calls for it (i.e. if someone's safety or well-being is at risk), it is perfectly right and sometimes necessary to share someone else's personal information.

- *Cool Q's*
  Why would someone gossip? What do we hope to accomplish when we gossip about others?
  Is it ever OK to share someone else's information? When?
  Is it possible that, if we share a friend's information for safety reasons, she will be upset with us? What should we do in those cases? How do we explain to her that we were not gossiping?

Group Discussion

"What is the difference between positive and negative criticism?"

- *The 411*
  This group discussion topic will help girls decipher between positive criticism that is meant to be constructive and negative criticism that is meant to cut people down.

- *Materials*
  Poster board
  Markers or pens

- *Instructions*
  Ask girls the question and allow them to freely provide their own answers and feelings on the topic. Record their answers on poster board. Use "Cool Qs" for further discussion.

- *Step Up!*
  Help the girls understand that distinguishing between good and bad criticism is essential. Constructively critical comments and suggestions can be difficult for someone to word properly; therefore, we can sometimes immediately become defensive and wind up misinterpreting positive criticism as negative. Encourage girls to pay attention to tone, body language, etc. when they hear these remarks. If they are still not sure, they should always ask the commenter what her intent was.

- *Cool Q's*
  How do you know when someone's comment is positive? Negative?
  Is there a way to make criticism positive?

Activity 16: Objection!

The 411

This exercise will help the girls determine, as objective outsiders, whether a comment was positive or negative, or whether a girl was gossiping or sharing information.

Instructions

This is a great improvisational activity to follow the previous discussion. Separate the girls into groups of four, and instruct them to create a story in which:

- A girl (the 'defense') made either a joking or taunting comment to a friend.
- A girl (the 'defense') gave either a positive or a negative criticism to a friend.
- A girl (the 'defense') either shared information or gossiped about a friend.
- These stories should be in line with the group discussions that prefaced this activity. Each group will act out a courtroom scene with each girl playing a different role in the trial (i.e. Judge, Lawyer, Witness, etc). The cases will follow their story ideas (e.g. The 'defense' said that another girl's boyfriend was "so much better than her last one"). The girls not in the group performing will act as the jury and determine whether the 'defense' had positive or negative intentions.

Cool Q's

- How did you come to this verdict?
- If you were in this situation in real life, would you view it, or the 'defense' any differently?

Shout Outs!

End the day by circling the girls up, and having the girls give "Shout Outs" to one another. Each girl should give at least one compliment or kudos for the day to every other girl. Thank the girls for coming.

Session 9

SEE WHAT I WANNA SEE:
Media Literacy

This session is meant to facilitate the girls' understanding of media imagery. By exploring film and television's portrayal of young women, they will learn how viewing these images can affect their own behavior and sense of self.

Group Check-In

Gather the girls into a comfortable circle or grouping and ask them about their week, how things are going at school; if there have been any issues lately, etc.

Free-Write

"Do you think media images of women are mainly positive or negative? Why? Give examples of each."

Whoosh!

Gather the girls in a circle. Select someone to begin and instruct her to either make a noise, a gesture, a movement or all three at the same time. As quickly as possible, each girl, starting to the right, will imitate her action(s) until her "Whoosh" goes all the way around the circle once. The next girl to the right will then create her own "Whoosh" and send it around the circle. This continues until everyone has the opportunity to create their own individual "Whoosh."

Group Discussion

"If we could change anything about the media, what would it be?"

- *The 411*
  This group discussion topic will help girls explore their feelings about media and media images of young women.

- *Materials*
  Poster board
  Markers or pens

SEE WHAT I WANNA SEE:
Media Literacy

- *Instructions*
  Ask girls the question and allow them to freely provide their own answers and feelings on the topic. Record their answers on poster board. Use "Cool Qs" for further discussion.

- *Cool Q's*
  What are some examples of television shows, advertisements, or movies that portray women and girls negatively?
  What are some examples of television shows, advertisements, or movies that portray women and girls positively?
  Do you think that it is possible to change the way the media portrays women? How do you think it could be done?

Activity 17: And Now a Word from Our Sponsors!

The 411

This exercise is designed to help girls understand the images that they see on television and to explore and discuss subliminal messaging.

Instructions

Ask the girls to separate themselves into groups of four or five. Each group will perform a commercial for any product of their choosing. They can invent their own or peform an existing commercial. The group first performs the advertisement as it would appear on television. Next, they should emphasize the subliminal, or hidden message of the advertisement. For example, if the commercial shows a woman receiving a vacuum cleaner for Christmas, she may respond "Thanks for the vacuum cleaner." In the second instance her response might be, "Thanks for the vacuum cleaner. I will need it since women were meant to stay in and clean houses."

Cool Q's

- What is a subliminal message? Can you think of some examples?
- How often do you think you see hidden or subliminal messages in advertising? Television? Movies?
- What kinds of hidden messages does the media put out?
- What effect do these messages have on us? On our self-images?

Activity 18: Theatrical Trailer

The 411

This activity challenges girls to think about how they wish the media in our country would change and what they think truly positive images of females look like.

Instructions

Separate the girls into groups of 3-5. Then, ask each group to come up with an idea for a movie (one that they create) that portrays women or girls in a healthy and positive way. Finally, have each group perform a trailer, or advertisement, for the movie.

Step Up!

This activity is a great opportunity for girls to show their creative sides. Make sure to go around to each group and help out with ideas (for example, maybe one person should do the voice-over, or narration, for the trailer while the others act it out).

Cool Q's

- How did these trailers portray women or girls positively?
- Do movies like these exist?
- If all movies portrayed women and girls as healthy and assertive, how might that affect the way we see ourselves?

Shout Outs!

End the day by circling the girls up, and having the girls give "Shout Outs" to one another. Each girl should give at least one compliment or kudos for the day to every other girl. Thank the girls for coming.

Session 10

HOW TO DEAL PT. 1:
Healing and Dealing

The How to Deal sessions are meant to assist you and your group in learning healthy conflict resolution skills. The girls will learn that although relational aggression is easy, it reaps tremendous consequences. Also, just because we are used to acting a specific way does not mean we are unable to change. It is your job, as group facilitator, to help lead the girls to this discovery during these final sessions.

Group Check-In

Gather the girls into a comfortable circle or grouping and ask them about their week, how things are going at school; if there have been any issues lately, etc.

Free-Write

"Have you ever not known how to confront a friend without making her upset? Have you ever felt uncomfortable apologizing for something?"

Whoosh!

Gather the girls in a circle. Select someone to begin and instruct her to either make a noise, a gesture, a movement or all three at the same time. As quickly as possible, each girl, starting to the right, will imitate her action(s) until her "Whoosh" goes all the way around the circle once. The next girl to the right will then create her own "Whoosh" and send it around the circle. This continues until everyone has the opportunity to create their own individual "Whoosh."

Activity 19: Pick-Up Lines!

The 411

This activity explores how girls and women tend to justify behaviors like gossiping, spreading rumors, saying something mean, etc. instead of being forthcoming with our feelings and confronting the situation with honesty.

Instructions

Have each girl write down her favorite movie line, quote, etc. on a piece of paper, and put these in a hat or a bowl. Two girls will create a scene about anything they wish, and at various points in the scene, they will stop what they are doing, pick up one of the papers, and read the line that is written. They will then have to justify saying this, and make it work in the scene-as crazy and nonsensical as the line may seem in that context. This activity will lead to a discussion on why we work extremely hard to hide or deny the negative things we say and do instead of just owning up to our behavior.

Cool Q's

- How did it feel to have to justify what you just said, and make it work in the scene?
- Has a friend ever found out that you said something about her, and instead of owning up to it, you tried to work around it? Justify it? Explain it by blaming someone else or making it seem like no big deal?
- Why do you think doing this is easier than being honest?

Activity 20: The Tough Stuff

Materials

Journals

"I Statements"

Instructions

In their journals, have girls write the phrase "I feel _____ when you _____." For example: "I feel hurt when you ignore me at school." Ask them to fill this in, as if they were confronting a friend about an issue. Then, explain the proactive, positive model of confronting someone:
- Affirm the friendship from the beginning.
- I –Statement should be given.
- Request whatever it is you need (e.g. an apology).
- Affirm the friendship one last time. This will help keep the person from becoming defensive or concerned over losing your relationship.

"Apology Letters"

Instructions

In their journals, ask girls to write an apology letter to someone in their life (past or present) whom they need to apologize to. Follow the model below:
- "I'm sorry." These should always be your first words.
- Explain what you are apologizing for. Just saying "I'm sorry" doesn't cut it; the
- other person needs to know what you are sorry for.
- Affirm the friendship. Always.

Activity 21: Every Other Line

The 411
This is a therapeutic role-playing exercise that is designed to help girls learn how to confront aggressors in a healthy and productive manner.

Instructions
Once both of the previous activities are completed, ask the girls to pair off. Then, have each pair come up and demonstrate the correct way to confront and to apologize to someone. The girls should use and perform their I-Statements from the previous activity in these scenes. The girl who is not reading the I-Statement should respond with an apology that follows the structure described in Activity 20. The girls should not be allowed time to rehearse these scenes, however. While one girl is reading, the other should be improvising her reaction and apology on-the-spot, therefore making her reactions as realistic as possible. Each girl should perform both a confrontation and an apology.

Step Up!
Encourage the girls to be as realistic and natural as possible. This will help you in the discussion.

Cool Q's
- How did it feel to confront someone that way? How did it feel to be confronted?
- How did apologizing feel?
- Do you think it is possible for girls to confront and apologize to one another this way?

At Home Activity
Ask each girl to prepare a short presentation on how she copes with friendship issues, fights, hurt feelings, etc. (i.e. by journaling, writing poetry, reading).

Shout Outs!
End the day by circling the girls up, and having the girls give "Shout Outs" to one another. Each girl should give at least one compliment or kudos for the day to every other girl. Thank the girls for coming.

Session 11

HOW TO DEAL PT.2:
Healing and Dealing

Group Check-In

Gather the girls into a comfortable circle or grouping and ask them about their week, how things are going at school; if there have been any issues lately, etc.

Free-Write

"If_____ (e.g. a fight, or problem) happens, I could talk to_____"
"Where in the school do you feel safe?"

Whoosh!

Gather the girls in a circle. Select someone to begin and instruct her to either make a noise, a gesture, a movement or all three at the same time. As quickly as possible, each girl, starting to the right, will imitate her action(s) until her "Whoosh" goes all the way around the circle once. The next girl to the right will then create her own "Whoosh" and send it around the circle. This continues until everyone has the opportunity to create their own individual "Whoosh."

At Home Activity (cont'd)

Have each girl give her At Home Activity presentations to the rest of the group.

Group Discussion

"What is the best way to cope with a problem? What are some effective coping mechanisms?"

The 411

This discussion, if done effectively, can help girls explore and realize various ways of handling problems, instead of getting mad and saying or doing things that they will regret later.

HOW TO DEAL PT.2:
Healing and Dealing (cont.)

Materials
Poster board
Markers or pens

Instructions
Ask girls the question and allow them to freely provide their own answers and feelings on the topic. Record their answers on poster board.

Step Up!
Make sure to suggest coping techniques such as venting in a journal or to a family member before directly confronting someone with anger. Also, it is helpful to write down the girls' suggestions on a poster board, as many of them might want to write the ideas down to use later.

Activity 22: Stay or Go?

The 411
This exercise helps girls discover the limits and boundaries in their friendships. It will also challenge girls' perceptions of what is acceptable and what is unacceptable in a healthy relationship.

Materials
Stay or Go?: Scenarios on page 69

Instructions
Read each scenario to the group. After each scenario, ask them whether they would stay in the friendship, or go. Make sure to ask why they feel that way, especially if there are disagreements.

Cool Q's
- What rights should you have as a friend?
- When should you say "enough is enough" in a friendship? What would be an example situation?
- Is it possible to accept a friend's apology but not wish to be friends with her anymore?

Final Project
Separate the girls into groups of 3-5. Each group must come up with a presentation that answers the question:

"What do I now know about friendships that I wish someone had told me when I was younger?"

The presentations can take the form of a skit, a poster presentation, artwork...the sky is the limit!

Step Up!
Make sure to go around the room and help each group with ideas for the Final Project.

Shout Outs!
End the day by circling the girls up, and having the girls give "Shout Outs" to one another. Each girl should give at least one compliment or kudos for the day to every other girl. Thank the girls for coming.

Session 12

WE'RE ALL IN THIS TOGETHER: *Saying Goodbye*

The final session focuses on two things: finishing the final group project, and leaving the girls with a feeling of teamwork and efficacy. The girls will feel closer, more intimate, and most importantly, more trusting.

Group Check-In

Gather the girls into a comfortable circle or grouping and ask them about their week, how things are going at school; if there have been any issues lately, etc. However, because this is the last session, encourage the girls to stick to lighter topics.

Final Project (cont'd)

Ask the girls to present their Final Project from the previous session to the rest of the group.

Cool Q's
- Who wishes that she had also learned this lesson earlier?
- Why is this lesson so important?

POST-PROGRAM SURVEYS

The 411
The post-program survey is designed to help you and your school measure the success of the program and the progress that the girls have made in their lives and feelings about relationships.

Materials
Post-Program Surveys on page 64
Pens, pencils

Instructions
Distribute a post-program survey to each girl. Collect the surveys when the group has finished.

Step Up!
Just like with the pre-program survey, make sure to encourage honesty!

Celebration/Goodbye!

Ask the girls to share one thing they gained from being in group, one thing they learned about each group member, and one thing that they admire in each group member. I recommend ending this last session with some kind of small celebration. I like to order a pizza, bring in some candy and soda, etc. This helps the girls feel a sense of closure for the program while also ending on a light, positive, and fun note.

Finally, thank the girls for all of their hard work and dedication over the past several weeks. Explain to them how much their honesty and participation meant to you. Distribute *Girls in the Lead* **Thank-You Cards.**

Optional Sessions

Optional Session 1

TAKING CARE OF BUSINESS PT.3: *An Exercise in Empathy*

The optional, third part of the Taking Care of Business sessions is meant to help girls explore the roles that bigotry and prejudice play in relational aggression. The activities are intended to help the group learn basic empathy, and to combat the use of derogatory slang and slur. This session is for older, developmentally mature girls. Sensitive and more intense issues will be discussed.

Group Check-In

Gather the girls into a comfortable circle or grouping and ask them about their week, how things are going at school; if there have been any issues lately, etc.

Free-Write

"Have you ever heard a girl put down another girl for being a different color or race? Have you ever heard a girl call another a girl a lesbian in an effort to get others to ignore her?" Explain.

Activity 23: Power Hop

The 411
This activity helps girls understand more about diversity and the role that prejudice plays in each of our lives.

Materials
Power Hop statements on page 70

Instructions
Have the group assemble on one side of the room. As you read each of the "Power Hop Statements" ask the girls to cross to the other side of the room if the statement applies to her. Each girl should return to the original side following each question.

Step Up!
This activity is very effective, but it can also make girls feel vulnerable. Usually intense, profound emotions are evoked. Therefore, make sure the girls know that the group is a safe space, and that although you encourage participation, everyone has the right to pass on a question. It will help to first explain why you are doing this activity. Make sure to discuss the importance and need for confidentiality as well.

Cool Q's
- What were you feeling during the exercise?
- How did it feel to be a part of a minority group? The majority?
- What is the role prejudice plays in our society?
- Did this change your understanding or personal definition of diversity?

Activity 24: What's in a Name?

The 411

This activity will help the girls begin to understand how the traits society values in girls (and therefore what girls strive to be like) conflict with what we associate with being homosexual. Girls call each other "gay" and "lesbian" in order to ostracize and relationally victimize one another. This exercise is designed to help girls understand the reasons they may bully one another based on perceived or actual sexual orientation and the emotional consequences of doing so.

Materials

3 Poster boards
Pens or markers

Instructions

On the first poster board, write the word "Girls." Hand out a marker or pen to each girl, and ask the group to think of traits that we, as a society, value in girls. Ask the girls to write these traits on the poster board. Write the word "Gay" on the second poster board, and "Straight" on the third. Ask the girls to brainstorm names, traits, and characteristics that they think describe each term and write them on the appropriate poster boards.

Cool Q's

- What are some differences between the traits society values in girls versus the traits we associate with being gay?
- Why would a girl call another girl "Gay" or "Lesbian" if she isn't one? What happens to that girl?
- How do you think it would feel if a girl started a rumor about your sexuality or sexual identity?
- How does this affect the way we treat people who actually are gay or lesbian?

Activity 25: Star Power

The 411

This activity encourages understanding and empathy for people of all sexual orientations, in an effort to prevent the use of homophobia in bullying.

Materials

Star Power cut-out on page 71
Pens or markers
Scissors

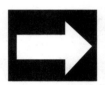

Instructions

Cut out and distribute a star to each girl. Ask them to number the "points" of the star, 1-5. Then, ask the girls to write the member of their family they are closest to on the first point, their favorite extra-curricular/school activity on the second point, their best friend's name on the third point, their dream job on the fourth point, and their dream house or place to live on the fifth point. Then, follow the steps and script below.

Explain that each star represents each girl's feeling of importance, purpose, and self-worth.

- Tell the girls that they just came out as gay or lesbian at school.
  Script: "Now that you have 'come out of the closet', your peers in your extra-curricular activity are 'weirded out' by you. Everyone please rip off your second point. You eventually feel so ignored and kicked out that you quit the program."

- Tell the girls that they just came out as gay or lesbian to their best friends.
  Script: "Now that you have told your friends that you are gay, some of you will keep your friends, but many of you will lose them. Many people, when 'coming out,' lose their best friends because they may be morally opposed to homosexuality or they just feel 'weirded out' by it. Please rip off your third point. You have lost your best friend."

- Tell the girls that they just came out as gay or lesbian to their closest family member.
  Script: "Now that you have told your closest family member that you are gay, some of you will keep that relationship, but many of you will lose it. Many gay youth are kicked out of their homes by family members upon 'coming out of the closet.' Many of these youth become homeless, just for being gay. Please rip off your first point. You have just lost your family."

- Tell the girls that they have just graduated college and are applying for their first job.
  Script: "Because you have decided to be open about your sexual orientation while applying for jobs, there is a strong chance that many employers will choose not to hire you just because you are gay. It is legal in most states in the U.S. to deny

someone a job based on his or her sexual orientation. Please rip off your fourth point. You have just been denied a job."

- Tell the girls that they are searching for an apartment, or house, in their favorite city or suburb.
  Script: "Because you have decided to be open about your sexual orientation while searching for a place to live, there is a strong chance that many real estate agents and sellers will refuse to sell you the house just because you are gay. It is legal in most states in the U.S. to deny someone housing based on his or her sexual orientation. Please rip off your fifth point. You have just been denied a house."

Step Up!
Like the other activities in this session, this one can bring up some extremely sensitive issues. Make sure that the girls feel safe and comfortable discussing these issues. Also, enforce the "respect" rule as much as possible here; many girls will laugh out of discomfort, therefore try to discourage this as much as possible.

Cool Q's
- How did this exercise make you feel?
- How did it feel each time you had to rip off a point of your star?
- What does your star look like now?
- After doing this activity, and being aware of the issues facing young gay people today, how do you think it feels to be made fun of for being gay?
- What does it mean to be accepting? Is it possible to accept someone as a human being even though we may disagree with what the person does?

Shout Outs!
End the day by circling the girls up, and having the girls give "Shout Outs" to one another. Each girl should give at least one compliment or kudos for the day to every other girl. Thank the girls for coming.

Optional Session 2

TTYL: *Saying 'Talk To You Later' to Cyberbullying*

As you probably know, the internet has become "the new bathroom wall." With services like AIM and Yahoo Messenger, along with sites such as Facebook, Myspace, Bebo, and Tag, gossip has become dangerously ubiquitous. The purpose of this optional session is to delve more deeply into the topic of gossip; specifically gossip that takes place (or is spread) via the internet. The idea the girls should walk away with is: if you wouldn't say it, don't click 'send.'

Group Check-In

Gather the girls into a comfortable circle or grouping and ask them about their week, how things are going at school; if there have been any issues lately, etc.

Free-Write

"What do you think the worst part, or consequence, of gossip is? How do you think gossip works on the internet?"

Whoosh!

Gather the girls in a circle. Select someone to begin and instruct her to either make a noise, a gesture, a movement or all three at the same time. As quickly as possible, each girl, starting to the right, will imitate her action(s) until her "Whoosh" goes all the way around the circle once. The next girl to the right will then create her own "Whoosh" and send it around the circle. This continues until everyone has the opportunity to create their own individual "Whoosh."

Activity 26: Freeze Frame

The 411
This activity is designed to help girls understand what gossip looks like and how it feels, but to also explore possible ways of combating the behavior.

Instructions
Separate the girls into two groups. Ask participants in Group 1 to 'mold' and 'sculpt' their bodies to create a complete, group image of "Gossip." This should look like a type of group statue (the girls will have to work together in order to make the image look like one piece). Ask Group 2 what they see in the image that was created. This is the Real Image. It represents how the girls, in actuality, view the topic. Group 1 will again form an image, but this time it will be what the girls think can be accomplished and changed about gossip. This is the ideal image. Again, have Group 2 respond and react to this image. Then start the entire activity over, with Group 2 forming the images.

Cool Q's
- What sort of image did Group 1(2) create?
- Do you think this is realistic?
- What are the different roles each girl is playing?
- What were the similarities between both groups' images?

Activity 27: Splat!

The 411

This exercise is designed to show the girls how much "easier" anonymous posting or messaging is compared to direct confrontation. This will help you lead a discussion on the consequences of taking that "easier" option, instead of the healthy, pro-active approach to relationships.

Materials

Poster board
Pens, markers, or pencils

Instructions

Hold up a piece of poster board (or attach it to you in some way), and explain to the girls that this is your "Facebook Wall." Then, ask the girls to think of something confrontational that they would typically want to say to a friend. Have each girl come up and write the statement down, in silence, on your "Facebook Wall." Call the girls back up, and take off the poster board. Ask the girls to look you directly in the eye and say what they just wrote on your "Facebook Wall" exactly, but this time, to you directly.

Cool Q's

- What was easier: writing on my wall, or talking to me directly?
- Were you uncomfortable when you had to confront me directly?
- Why do you think it is easier to write mean comments, or gossip, on the internet? What are the consequences of doing so?

Activity 28: Mano-a-Mano

The 411
This activity is intended to help the girls realize how much bigger conflict and confrontation become if they occur on the internet versus in person. The girls in the pair will suffer through miscommunications and frustration before something, if anything, gets resolved.

Instructions
Separate girls into pairs, and have each pair come up to the performance area one at a time. Ask the pair to act out an Instant Message conversation, in which one of them confronts the other over an issue (e.g. she spread a rumor, she flirted with her boyfriend, she didn't invite her friend to her party, etc.). Allow the girls to choose. Before the pair acts out the conversation, have the girls turn their backs to each other, and mime typing throughout the entire performance (this way, they cannot see each other).

Cool Q's
- Were there any miscommunications in the scenes?
- How much harder is it to resolve conflict on the internet, versus in person?
- If we know it is harder, why would we still choose to confront our friends on IM?
- Instead of using the internet, what are other options when your feelings are hurt, or you want to confront a friend? How much better are these options?

Shout Outs!
End the day by circling the girls up, and having the girls give "Shout Outs" to one another. Each girl should give at least one compliment or kudos for the day to every other girl. Thank the girls for coming.

BEST OF BOTH WORLDS?:
Exploring Sexual Violence, Sexuality, and Stigma

This session is designed to help the girls talk about some of the most sensitive, difficult topics of their young adulthood: sexual violence, sexuality, and stigma. This session is intended for girls who are not only old enough and mature enough to handle the topic, but who will reap the most benefit out of these activities and discussions. It is of utmost importance for you to help the girls feel safe and supported while doing the following activities. Again, stress trust, support, and confidentiality among group members.

Group Check-In

Gather the girls into a comfortable circle or grouping and ask them about their week, how things are going at school; if there have been any issues lately, etc.

Activity 29: Reputation
Heads Up 7 Up

Instructions

Ask the girls to put their heads down and close their eyes. Ask the following questions, and instruct the girls to raise their hands if their answer is "yes."

- Have you ever heard a girl call another girl a "slut?"
- Have you ever heard a girl call another girl a "slut" as a joke?
- Have you ever been called the word "slut"?
- Have you ever used the word "slut" to describe another girl?
- Do you know anyone who was sexually harassed by a boy?
- Do you feel like girls need to stand up for themselves more in relationships?
- Do you think that relationships can be dangerous?
- Do you think that being the target of sexual harassment, abuse, or rape can ruin a girl's reputation?

Activity 30: Makin' Faces 2

The 411

This activity explores the negative stigma that we, as females, give to instances of date rape, sexual harassment, and sexual abuse. Most of the groups of three will start to treat the fourth girl differently once they find out that she was a victim.

Materials

Makin' Faces 2: Scenarios on page 72
Hat or bowl
Scissors

Instructions

Cut-out and place Makin' Faces 2 scenarios into the hat or bowl. Have girls separate into groups of four and go up to the performance area one at a time. The group will pick out one slip of paper from "the hat." Have three of the girls read the slip, but do not allow the fourth girl to see it.

The setting will be a lunchroom, and the three girls will be sitting at a table while the fourth enters and sits down with the rest of the clique. Allow the girls to create their own, completely improvised scene, and watch what happens with the rest of your audience.

Ask the fourth girl how she is feeling: Is she angry? Upset? Does she think the other girls are mad at her? Does she feel ostracized, or does she feel supported? Do the same with each group. At the very end, read the slips aloud to the entire group.

Cool Q's

- How did the groups of three feel after reading the slips?
- How did the cliques wind up treating their friends?
- Is that how you think the rest of the school would treat her, were they to find out?
- Why do you think we might not be supportive of girls and women who are victims of sexual violence?
- Have you ever heard someone say "well, she was 'asking for it'"? What does that mean? Do you think that is right?

Activity 31: Dating Bill of Rights

The 411
This exercise challenges girls to think about what rights and protections they would like to have in romantic relationships.

Materials
Poster board
Pens or markers
Dating Bill of Rights handout on page 73

Instructions
Distribute a Dating Bill of Rights to each girl. Ask girls to brainstorm and write down their own list of rights on their handout. Encourage them to think of rights that will ensure their safety and happiness while in a romantic relationship. Once they have finished completing their individual Dating Bill of Rights, ask girls to combine their ideas into a Group Dating Bill of Rights. Girls should write their ideas down on the poster board. Once the Group Dating Bill of Rights is completed, ask the group members to sign their names at the bottom.

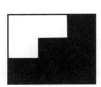

Step Up!
Encourage the girls to be as absolutely honest as possible; be sure to remind them that you will not scold anyone for her beliefs or values. Encourage this same respect with the rest of the group.

Cool Q's
- Why are these rights important?
- Why is safety important in romantic and dating relationships?
- Do you feel as though you have these rights? Do you feel as though you can assert these rights if you were in a relationship?
- Why might it be hard for a girl to assert her rights in a relationship? Does this mean she is weak?

Shout Outs!
End the day by circling the girls up, and having the girls give "Shout Outs" to one another. Each girl should give at least one compliment or kudos for the day to every other girl. Thank the girls for coming.

Pre- and Post- Program Survey

Girls can bully each other just like boys can.
   ❏ **Yes**   ❏ **No**

I am 100% capable of being a true, loyal friend to other girls, at all times.
   ❏ **Yes**   ❏ **No**   ❏ **Maybe**

I know how to handle a fight with a friend so that neither of us will get hurt.
   ❏ **Yes**   ❏ **No**   ❏ **Maybe**

I always confront another girl, or a friend, if I am having an issue with her.
   ❏ **Yes**   ❏ **No**   ❏ **Maybe**

If I told my friend a secret, I know she'd keep it private.
   ❏ **Yes**   ❏ **No**   ❏ **Maybe**

If my friend told me a secret, I know I'd keep it private.
   ❏ **Yes**   ❏ **No**   ❏ **Maybe**

Whenever I see a girl being mean to another girl, I try and do something to stop it.
   ❏ **Yes**   ❏ **No**   ❏ **Maybe**

Sometimes I feel like staying home from school because I don't want to see other girls.
   ❏ **Yes**   ❏ **No**   ❏ **Maybe**

I like to talk to my friends on the internet (AIM, Yahoo Messenger, Facebook, Myspace, Bebop, Tag) and sometimes this can lead to drama.
   ❏ **Yes**   ❏ **No**   ❏ **Maybe**

Sometimes I feel like teachers don't do enough to help us when we're having friend fights.
   ❏ **Yes**   ❏ **No**   ❏ **Maybe**

Sometimes I feel like my family doesn't do enough, or doesn't know what to do to help me when I'm having an issue with another girl.
   ❏ **Yes**   ❏ **No**   ❏ **Maybe**

There is a difference between good and bad gossip.
   ❏ **Yes**   ❏ **No**   ❏ **Maybe**

If I know a friend is mad at me, I will talk to other friends first before I confront her about the situation.
   ❏ **Yes**   ❏ **No**   ❏ **Maybe**

I have someone I could go to if I were feeling hurt or alone.
   ❏ **Yes**   ❏ **No**   ❏ **Maybe**

Group Evaluation Form

Did you enjoy your time in Girls in the Lead?
    ❑ **Yes**   ❑ **No**

Did you learn anything new?
    ❑ **Yes**   ❑ **No**

If so, what? _____

The best part of Girls in the Lead was _____

_____

My least favorite part of Girls in the Lead was _____

_____

Was the group leader helpful?
    ❑ **Yes**   ❑ **No**

What is the most important thing you learned in group? _____

_____

_____

Did you like journaling?
    ❑ **Yes**   ❑ **No**

Did you like the theatre activities?
    ❑ **Yes**   ❑ **No**

Would you recommend Girls in the Lead to other girls?
    ❑ **Yes**   ❑ **No**

Overall, Girls in the Lead was…
    ❑ **Not helpful**   ❑ **Alright**   ❑ **Really helpful!**

Jingo Bingo Sheet

Find someone who has more than 4 siblings	Find someone who has more than one pet	Find someone who has traveled outside of the U.S.	Find someone who watches at least one reality TV show
Find someone who sings in a choir or plays an instrument in a band	Find someone who has gone to see a live concert	Find someone who has been to overnight or summer camp	Find someone whose favorite season is winter
Find someone who likes fashion magazines	Find someone whose favorite sport is basketball	Find someone who has an older sister	Find someone who has kept the same friends all her life
Find someone who has changed friend groups throughout her life	Find someone who likes solving math and science problems	Find someone who likes to dance around the house when no one is watching	Find someone who knows where she wants to go to college

The Best Girl for the Job: Questionnaire

I tend to have an "alternative" style when it comes to my clothes. If I choose you as a friend, would you let me wear whatever clothes I wanted?

_____

As much as I'm sure I'll enjoy my friendship with you, I do have other friends. If I choose you as a friend, would you be okay with me hanging out with other people without you at times?

_____

I'll admit it: I really love junk food. If I choose you as a friend, would I be able to have whatever sized-body I want? Or would I have to wear a specific size?

_____

I really like science and math, and I'm thinking about trying-out for the math team. If I choose you as a friend, would you let me participate in whatever activities I wanted?

_____

As I said before, I'm kind of a nerd, and I tend to get straight-A's. If I choose you as a friend, would you care what grades I was getting?

_____

I like to have my social butterfly moments. I think that having as many different friends as possible is great! Variety is the spice of life, right? If I choose you as a friend, would I be able to sit at different lunch tables from time-to-time?

_____

I tend to have crushes on people who aren't exactly considered cool or popular. If I choose you as a friend, would you care who I dated or what the person looks like?

_____

I think that drama should be left on the stage. Let's say you were in a fight with a mutual friend of ours. If I choose you as a friend, would you expect me to treat this girl badly? Or ignore her like you might be?

_____

Makin' Faces 1: Scenarios

Last night you had a fight with your mom over the chores you have (but haven't been doing) around the house. She is making you stay in this next weekend instead of going to that party you were looking forward to.

You didn't do so hot on your last math test, and your dad found out. He just grounded you for three weeks.

You didn't make the part in the school play that you really wanted.

You didn't make the spot on the basketball team that you have been looking forward to all year.

Your coach just cut you from the Varsity track and field team down to the Junior Varsity.

Your best friend was just grounded by her parents, and now she can't go out this weekend.

You and your boyfriend just broke up last night on the internet, and you have yet to talk to him.

Stay or Go?: Scenarios

Your friend jokingly called you a "loser" at lunch today. **Stay or Go?**

Your friend purposely did not save you a seat in math class today, even though you have sat next to each other all year. **Stay or Go?**

Your friend let someone take your seat at the lunch table. **Stay or Go?**

Your friend ignored you all day, without telling you why. When you tried to talk to her, she just walked away. **Stay or Go?**

Your friend told another one of your close friends that you were gossiping about her (the close friend). You know that this isn't true, but now she isn't talking to you. **Stay or Go?**

Your friend convinced your group to ignore you all day, for no apparent reason. This has happened several times before. **Stay or Go?**

Your friend convinced your group to ignore you for an entire week, for no apparent reason. This has happened several times before. You keep asking your friend to stop, but she never seems to listen. **Stay or Go?**

Your friend spread a cruel rumor about you and a boy. Now it feels like the entire school is talking about it. **Stay or Go?**

Your friend purposely flirted with your crush in front of you. **Stay or Go?**

Your friend invited everyone else to her birthday party except you. When you asked her about it, she said that she didn't want you to "weird" out her other friends. **Stay or Go?**

Your friend somehow found your password on Facebook and Myspace. She logged onto your account and flamed your wall with cruel messages, and changed some of your personal settings to say nasty and embarrassing things about you. When you confronted her about this, she said she was just angry with you. **Stay or Go?**

Your friend started a hate petition about you at school. Again, she justified this by saying she was just angry with you, and she was "letting off steam." **Stay or Go?**

Power Hop Statements

- You are a woman.

- You identify as Asian, Southeast Asian, East Indian, or Pacific Islander.

- You identify as Latina or Chicano.

- You identify as African American, Black, or of African descent.

- You identify as Caucasian.

- You are Jewish.

- You are Muslim.

- You are Hindu.

- You are Christian.

- You are of a multi-ethnic background.

- You do not know your ethnic background.

- You were once told that you did not act "black enough."

- You were once told that you did not act "white enough."

- You were once discriminated against based on your color, religion, or background.

- You come from a single parent household.

- You are a single parent.

- Your native language is not English.

- You once felt racial tension in a situation, but were afraid to say anything.

- You once heard anti-gay slurs, but were afraid to say anything.

- You once heard anti-Muslim or anti-Arab slurs, but were afraid to say anything.

- You once heard anti-black slurs, but were afraid to say anything.

- You know someone who identifies themself as gay or lesbian.

- You have been called gay or lesbian, in a derogatory manner.

- You are sometimes uncomfortable changing in front of others, such as in a locker room.

- You once felt uncomfortable in a group because you were the only one of your race/color/creed/ethnicity/religion/sexual identity.

Star Power Cut-Out

There are rumors going around school that Girl 4 was date raped at the party over the weekend.

You have heard a rumor that Girl 4 was the first person in your school to lose her virginity.

Your friends just told you that Girl 4 hooked up with some older college student that she did not know over the weekend.

There are rumors being spread around the school that Girl 4 might be pregnant.

Dating Bill of Rights | Activity Sheet

I, as a young woman, hereby declare the inalienable rights I must have in any romantic relationship. I understand that I must assert these rights at all times, in all situations, in order to ensure my safety and happiness in the relationship.

1. _____

2. _____

3. _____

4. _____

5. _____

6. _____

7. _____

8. _____

9. _____

10. _____

Clique Break-Down

Queen Bee

Wannabe

Bystanders and Targets
(these can often be interchangeable)

Alternate Activities

Warm-Ups and Ice-Breakers

Do You Like Your Neighbor?

Standing in a circle, pick someone to stand in the middle. That person walks up to anyone and asks them "Do You Like Your Neighbor?" If that person answers "NO" the two people on either side of her must swap spaces while the person in the middle tries to get one of the spaces. Who ever is left without a space is "it." If that person answers "YES...I like my neighbor, but I really like people who (fill-in the blank)." It could be anything from... "Yes, but I really like people who have braces or are wearing a certain color..." Be creative!!! Everyone who fits the criteria then moves about the circle and must find a new space. Again, the person left without a space goes to the middle of the circle, and it starts again.

Hot Spot – An Advanced Game

Standing in a circle, one player steps into the middle and starts singing a known song. As soon as this player shows any signs of stopping (because she doesn't know the lines any more, gets tired or embarrassed) another player needs to step in and take over (singing a different song). This exercise is not about improvising songs, but more of a group thing. Players need to know that the group will support them when they're out of breath. The idea is to keep singing. Singing can be replaced with dancing.

Improv

Day in the Life

Have a girl recall a time when she was bullied/ saw a friend being bullied. The other girls then act out the scene, with a discussion of the events to follow.

3 Genres

This is an extraordinarily fun game to play, and it will really help to get those creative juices flowing. Ask 2-3 girls to act out a scene about bullying or Relational Aggression. Then, have them perform the scene again in a different genre (Western, Horror, Romantic Comedy, etc.). You can do as many genres as you wish.

Support Group

Three players attend a meeting run by the fourth, for their strange addiction. In this case, the three players will each represent a different role a girl can play in a clique and will talk about why they are having trouble getting out of those roles, and/or the clique itself. The leader will help them explore this.

The Jerry Oprah Show

Same idea as before, except in a talk-show, "Oprah" type format. The host can help the girls sort out their issues, or conflict, interviewing each one individually and then as a group.

Theatre and Misc.

Anonymous Advice

This is a great, non-theatre activity to engage in if you sense that some of the girls are having friendship difficulties. On a piece of paper, the girls write down whatever issue they are going through, why it is difficult, etc. These papers should remain anonymous. Then, as a group leader, you will go through the papers one-by-one, paraphrasing what was written to the rest of the group. The girls can then discuss what they would do in that situation, what is realistic, what is idealistic, etc.

Pushing It

The girls stand in pairs, facing each other, and place their hands on each other's shoulders. Ask the girls to imagine a line between them, and then to start pushing each other. When one girl feels that her 'adversary' is weaker, have her ease off so she doesn't cross the line. If one girl increases her strength, the other must as well, as the goal is to not cross the line. Following the activity, lead a discussion about how this represents balance in our relationships; how we must not hold power over our friends if they are weaker, or more insecure, and that we must constantly be aware of when to intervene, when to confront each other, how to do so, etc.

Aristotle

This activity is great for building trust and group dynamic. One girl stands in the middle of the circle, and starts a movement or creates a pose. Everyone else must help her complete this image. For example, if she mimes typing, other girls should form the computer, keyboard, mouse, etc. Feel free to have 2-3 circles going at the same time, depending on the size of the group.

Your A, B, C's

Girls form a circle. One at a time, they go into the middle and express a feeling, emotion, or idea using only the sound of the letter "A" (along with any gestures or movements they may choose). Then another goes in and expresses a different idea, emotion, or feeling with "E." Go through "A," "E," "I," "O," and "U." Once everyone has had a chance to be in the middle, have the girls begin again using a word starting with "A," then "E," and so on. Finally, allow them to use a sentence starting with the exact letter.

Our Body

This is a great exercise to do at the beginning of the program, as it will help you understand more about the girls as individuals. Hand out a piece of paper and pencil to each girl, and ask her to draw a picture of herself, with her eyes closed. Let the group know that they can put anything they want to in the picture, and that they have "free range" over their portraits (this way, girls, if they want, can add objects, clothes, other people, etc.). Collect the pictures and arrange them in a random order on the floor, and ask the girls to open their eyes. Ask what strikes them most about the drawings- did the girls focus on their bodies? How much detail? Did they add in any interests (i.e. a tennis racquet, etc.) or other people?

GIRLS IN THE LEAD

Certificate of Completion

This certifies that

_____

has successfully completed the *Girls in the Lead* program.

Congratulations on all of your hard work and accomplishments! Girls in the Lead would not be the same without you!

_____   _____
Date   Group Leader Signature

THANK YOU!

Dear _____

_____

_____

_____

_____

_____

_____

Sincerely,

_____

Date _____

Bibliography and Recommended Reading

Baker, Jean M. *How Homophobia Hurts Children: Nurturing Diversity at Home, at School, and in the Community*. New York: Harrington Park Press, 2002.

Bjorkqvist, Kaj, and Pirkko Niemela, eds. *Of Mice and Women: Aspects of Female Aggression*. San Diego: Academic Press, 1992.

Bosworth, Kris, Dorothy L. Espelage, and Thomas R. Simon. "Factors Associated With Bullying Behavior in Middle School Students." *Journal of Early Adolescence* 19, no. 3 (1999): 341-62.

Brown, Lyn Mikel. *Raising Their Voices: The Politics of Girls' Anger*. Cambridge, MA: Harvard University Press, 1998.

Brown, Lyn Mikel, and Carol Gilligan. *Meeting at the Crossroads: Women's Psychology and Girls' Development*. Cambridge, MA: Harvard University Press, 1992.

Brumberg, Joan Jacobs. *The Body Project: An Intimate History of American Girls*. New York: Vintage, 1997.

Davis, Angela Y. *Women, Race, and Class*. New York: Vintage, 1981.

Dellasega, Cheryl. *Surviving Ophelia: Mothers Share Their Wisdom in Navigating the Tumultuous Teenage Years*. Cambridge, MA: Perseus, 2001.

Evans-Winters, Venus E. *Teaching Black Girls: Resiliency in Urban Classrooms*. New York, NY: Peter Lang Publishing, 2005.

Freedman, Judy S. *Easing the Teasing: Helping Your Child Cope with Name-Calling, Ridicule, and Verbal Bullying*. New York, NY: Contemporary Books, 2002.

Garbarino, James. *See Jane Hit: Why Girls Are Growing More Violent and What We Can Do About It*. New York: The Penguin Press, 2006.

Gilligan, Carol. *In a Different Voice: Psychological Theory and Women's Development*. Cambridge, MA: Harvard University Press, 1982.

Hewitt, Roger. *White Talk, Black Talk: Inter-Racial Friendship and Communication Amongst Adolescents*. Cambridge; New York: Cambridge University Press, 1986.

Irvine, Janice M., ed. *Sexual Cultures and the Construction of Adolescent Identities*. Philadelphia: Temple University Press, 1994.

Jack, Dana Crowley. *Silencing the Self: Women and Depression*. Cambridge, MA: Harvard University Press, 1991.

Kilbourne, Jean. *Deadly Persuasion: Why Women and Girls Must Fight the Addictive Power of Advertising*. New York: Free Press, 1999.

Levenkron, Steven. *Cutting: Understanding and Overcoming Self-Mutilation*. New York, NY: W.W. Norton and Company, 1998.

Levy, Ariel. *Female Chauvinist Pigs: Women and the Rise of Raunch Culture*. New York, NY: Free Press, 2005.

Lopez, Nancy. Hopeful Girls, Troubled Boys: Race and Gender Disparity in Urban Education. New York, NY: Routledge, 2003.

Orenstein, Peggy. *Schoolgirls: Young Women, Self-Esteem, and the Confidence Gap*. New York: Doubleday, 1994.

Pipher, Mary. *Reviving Ophelia: Saving the Selves of Adolescent Girls*. New York: Ballantine, 1995.

Sadker, Myra, and David Sadker. *Failing at Fairness: How America's Schools Cheat Girls*. New York: Scribner's, 1994.

Simmons, Rachel. *Odd Girl Out: The Hidden Culture of Aggression in Girls*. Orlando, FL: Harcourt Books, 2002.

Taylor, Jill McLean, Carol Gilligan, and Amy M. Sullivan. *Between Voice and Silence: Women and Girls, Race and Relationship*. Cambridge, MA: Harvard University Press, 1995.

Wiseman, Rosalind. *Queen Bees and Wannabes: Helping Your Daughter Survive Cliques, Gossip, Boyfriends, and other Realities of Adolescence*. New York: Crown Publishers, 2002.

Wolf, Naomi. *Promiscuities: The Secret Struggle for Womanhood*. New York: Ballantine, 1997.

Yalom, Irvin D. *The Theory and Practice of Group Psychotherapy*. Basic Books, 1970.

About the Author

Alissa Norby works as a Relational Aggression Consultant for the Chicago Public School system, where she serves several regions each year and does work for the Girls' Initiative project. She is the creator of *Girls in the Lead*, a unique theatre-based program for the intervention and prevention of female bullying. Alissa studied adolescent female psychology and drama therapy at Mount Holyoke College and she continues to do research on adolescent female psychology in Illinois with the Chicago School of Professional Psychology and the public school system. She has worked with and brought her innovative approach to bullying to several organizations, including the Girl Scouts of Chicago, Helping Girls Navigate Adolescence, ChildServ, YWCA and YMCA camps, Chicago Communities in Schools, Center on Halsted's Young Women's Program, Teen Living Program, the PACT Adolescent Caucus, and the Chicago After-School Matters program. Her work with adolescents has been spotlighted in a number of publications and media, including *Teen Vogue, Mother Jones, The Advocate, Curve Magazine, Chicago Tribune, Chicago Sun-Times, Fox News, WBEZ Chicago,* and the *Speak Up* radio broadcast in NYC. In addition to her work in psychology, Alissa has been trained in theatre performance and instruction at the Second City, Improv Olympic, and the Annoyance Theatre. She currently works with the council for the Chicago Girls' Initiative, the Children's Project team, the Young Women's Leadership Committee (under the Chicago Foundation for Women), the Illinois Safe Schools Alliance, and the House Theatre of Chicago.